Unp

A Journey of Letting Go

By Amy Lauer

Thank you!
To my unofficial editor :) !

"I can't give you a surefire formula for success, but I can give you a formula for failure: try to please everybody all the time."

- Herbert Bayard Swope [1]

Foreword

What you hold in your hands is a simple journal entry. Well, a journal entry that turned into a few chapters. And when chapters are bound and sold, I'm told it is a book. So here it is. My first book. I guess that makes me an author!

This book is half research and half me-search, exploring why and how stress impacts our lives so drastically. It is my first attempt at understanding a piece of myself that I believe is also present within a majority of people in our culture of perfection. If you are like me, I hope these chapters help you to identify the sources of your struggle so you too can begin the journey of letting go.

As it is my first attempt, if you find unperfection in this book, that's ok. That's kind of the point.

So let's get started.

*Names have been changed to protect confidentiality

Preface

Anxiety. Stress. Worry. Depression. The occurrence of these vices has risen for decades. [2] For some, this also means that the incidence of spa days, essential oil usage, and yoga practice also increases. But not for all. Many of us simply accept these characteristics as facts of life. We tell ourselves that everyone feels this way, and thus we are convinced that these feelings are "normal".

There are plenty of explanations as to why we feel this way. One study purports that depression is an attribute only of the modern era. The author states that, "Modern populations are increasingly overfed, malnourished, sedentary, sunlight-deficient, sleep-deprived, and socially-isolated." [3] There you have it. To some extent, we seem to be doing this to ourselves.

What causes this huge influx of stress and anxiety that we are seeing in our world recently? While scientists point to a myriad of influences, I have a singular theory: perfectionism.

All my life I believed that perfectionism was the answer to my problems. If I got everything in my life to be perfect, then I'd be happy. But living this way only proved the opposite to be true. By trying to make everything in my life perfect, I only became more dissatisfied. I realized that I was missing out on a lot of joyful experiences and beautiful people and because I was searching for my own personal paradise. Instead of gaining what I wanted, perfectionism was stealing what I loved.

Perfectionism does much more harm than it does good. You may not believe this now, but I hope that by the end of this book, you do. I hope that you can see that there are avenues other than striving for perfection that reap better and more lasting rewards. And I hope that you choose those avenues instead, like I've started to.

Starting in middle school, stress and anxiety were not only normal to me, but ingrained into my daily life. Because of this, it took years for me to notice them, let alone begin the journey to conquering them.

At the time, these vices didn't even seem negative. Worrying seemed like a necessity to hedge against the bad. I told myself, "If I worry about it now, I will be prepared for it later, and that's a good thing," not realizing the huge toll it was taking on my physical and mental state.

The physical symptoms arose during my Junior year of high school. I suppose this internal conflict had been building up for years, but my body finally had enough. This is when the "stomach attacks" began. Sometimes they were mild, but often they required me to lay down for hours without moving. Twice I required a hospital visit, and one time in a foreign country.

We searched for answers for years. Multiple gastroenteroloy appointments, three prescriptions, two colonoscopies, and one allergist recommendation later, the answer came: Irritable Bowel Syndrome (IBS). Which just means they don't actually know what is wrong with you.

Melanie and I walked through the entrance to the indoor pool. Christian and his dad followed behind us. I was so glad for some exercise, as the past few days had been full of sitting and eating. But, what else would you expect from Christmas in Germany?

My first time in Germany was four years prior—during the Summer of 2009— when I was a German exchange student through a program at my high school. Melanie and I were matched, along with her cousin, Monika, and my best friend, Ariel. That first summer together we had tons of adventures, and this time around was no different. Except, instead of going to school for six weeks to learn German, now I was on vacation for three weeks to have fun.

This was my first time away from home for Christmas, but Melanie's and Monika's families welcomed me. Ariel and her family —who I affectionately called my second family—had also come along, so I felt as close to home as possible.

After the Christmas celebrations, Melanie and I spent some time in her apartment a few villages away. We met up with Christian and Fritz, who were Melanie's high school classmates, and mine during that Summer of 2009. Though we hadn't talked in years, we all got along splendidly again. In fact, we spent a straight week together. We went to the pool, explored the city of Marburg at night, played games, watched movies, and talked for hours. When it came time for me to leave, Christian and Fritz wrote me a song called, "American Amy". It was such a special three weeks.

But this particular day was about to be infamous.

It started out as another pool day. When I jumped in, I instantly felt joy. I missed swimming. As a kid, I went to our neighborhood pool as often as I could. Now that I was in college, I didn't make time for it. Being here, I resolved that I wouldn't forgo this love of mine for so long. I'd swim more.

We were only swimming for a bit before I felt sick. I excused myself, thinking that the nausea would pass. Maybe I just had too much to eat the night before.

I made my way to a locker room stall and closed the door. Sitting down on the bench, I put my head in my hands. I tried to take deep breaths and wait until the nausea passed, but it didn't. I wanted to go find Melanie and tell her we had to go, but I couldn't move. I also hated making people change their plans for me.

So I waited.

And waited.

After what seemed like a long time, I heard the door open and Melanie's voice called, "Amy?"

"Yeah? I'm feeling really sick. I think we need to go."

"Ok. Let me go get our stuff,"

All I could do was sit and wait for her. She gathered our things and we prepared to leave.

I was able to stand up, but as I walked out of the locker room, my body started to go numb. First my arms, then my legs. And that's when I collapsed.

I fell to the floor, truly unable to move.

"Amy!"

"I'm numb. I can't feel anything," I garbled through my sobs as the tingling spread to my mouth.

There was some commotion, then the paramedics came. I was loaded onto a stretcher and taken to an ambulance.

"Where are you from?" One of the paramedics asked.

"United States," I managed.

"Don't worry, we are going to take care of you. You are going to be ok,"

"Ok,"

Once we got to the hospital he put his hand on me and said, "God be with you,"

Later, Melanie told me, "That's really unique. Most Germans do not talk about religion to strangers."

Stress is a plague. It rolls in, often without warning, and stays much longer than it should. It gives us ailments and diseases, it covers us in delirium, and it ultimately disorients our sense of reality. Unfortunately, it takes even longer to eradicate.

At the time, I believed those stomach attacks were related to something physical, but the reality was much deeper than that. After comparing my symptoms against others, and going to countless doctors appointments only to leave with no answers, I believe that these instances weren't IBS related. They were panic attacks.

Searching for a cure to my physical symptoms was the first time I learned about stress management. Before, the concept was foreign to me. I just believed that stress was part of life. But it isn't.

In fact, it's only recently that I've learned why I've lived so long with it, and how to finally live without it.

Riddance

I went down the basement stairs. "There can't be that much down here," I thought, "I moved out six years ago,"

I walked across the deep green carpet that my dad put down when he finished half of the basement so many years ago. He planned to finish the whole thing, but time didn't allow for it. So instead, the back section was purely storage. As a master organizer, my dad labeled all the containers and sectioned them into their appropriate spots: Yarn. Sewing. Christmas. DVDs. Ornaments. Books. Little X-mas Tree. Mums' X-mas Tree. X-mas Wreath.

Then, there was my section: Amy's Closet. Amy's Off-Season. Amy's Off-Season 2.0. Amy's Books. Amy's Schoolwork. Amy's Bedding. Amy's X-mas Tree.

There must've been 20 containers worth! Some large, some small, but all containing items which I simply didn't need, or even want. And that's when the purging began.

I knew that my mom might want some items for sentimental purposes, which is how I ended up with at least half of my stuff to begin with. I also knew that some of the items might be worth something, but I didn't want to invest in eBay. My mom previously mentioned wanting to sell a few items of her own, so I piled everything on the ping pong table for her to sort through.

I saved so many of those items for the perfect occasion or the perfect person. Or the perfect situation in which I would need my essays from 5th grade or my bed sheets from college. But, in the past six years, all of these perfect items went unused. So, was my perfect saving method really doing me any good, or was it actually robbing me of mental space, energy, and time?

By the time I was finished, half of the ping pong table was covered. It took two decades for me to acquire some of these items and two seconds for me to part with them. And it got me thinking, what else do I have that I don't actually care about?

It turned out to be a lot.

That trip home cracked open my understanding of how living with less gives you more of what you truly want. This revelation has been an integral part of my healing from perfectionism and I've learned that there's more to purge than just things: Emotions. Friendships. Ideals. Discontentment.

You may be familiar with the book that came out in 2014: "The Life Changing Magic of Tidying Up." In it, author Marie Kondo describes how the simple act of organizing can tremendously improve your quality of life. Or maybe you know of The Minimalists, Joshua Fields Millburn and Ryan Nicodemus. Maybe you watched their documentary on Netflix, read their book, followed the blog, or listened to the podcast. Maybe, like me, you were inspired by them to rid yourself of the unnecessary. Or maybe you thought, "I could never live like that. I love my stuff too much." If that's the case, let me remind you: minimalism is an individual journey. Find your starting point, and allow it to take you where you need to go.

Because the truth is, there is a balance between the stuff you have and the life that you live. If you have too little, you feel unfulfilled. If you have too much, you feel overwhelmed. And everyone's sweet spot is different. So instead of trying to attain

someone else's, find your own. There is no perfect.

Donate

Once I started getting rid of stuff, the hardest part was finding it a new home. I didn't have many items of extrinsic value, but I had lots of pieces with intrinsic value, and those are the hardest of all to part with. So, to lessen the blow, I would try to find someone who I knew could use it. When that failed, I would go to Goodwill.

This is where I went to drop off my old bike, Bree. He was named after the horse in "The Horse and His Boy" by C.S Lewis, one of my favorite books from "The Chronicles of Narnia" series.

Bree was my faithful companion all throughout college. I didn't have a car until my Senior year and so Bree took me everywhere: class, the grocery store, parties, the climbing wall. Bree was originally my dad's and so already had lots of miles, stories, and memories accumulated. I loved that bike so much that it took me over a year to get "rid" of it. When we were getting ready to move, my husband, Adam, suggested taking it down to the dumpster. But I couldn't part with Bree that way. I had to find someone that would love him. Or I had to at least take him to Goodwill.

So off I went. I used my old U-lock to keep the wheels in place on the bike rack while I drove. Well, since it was snowing, the U-lock froze. When I got to Goodwill, the employee tried to unlock it, but ended up breaking the key instead. Now I was literally stuck with Bree.

My only option was to find an electric saw to cut the U-lock. I ran to The Home Depot to see how much they were. I called friends to see if I could borrow one. No luck. I began to worry. I began to shake with stress. My stomach started knotting; this is the first sign of a stomach attack. And to stop that cycle I have to calm down. I have to take deep breaths. So I did. As my body calmed, so did my mind. And then it hit me: I lived in an apartment complex with 24-hour maintenance. I quickly called the front desk to see if one of their employees had an electric saw. They did. I drove over to meet up with the guy who could help me.

The man's name was Angel.

Once the U-lock was sawed off, I went back to Goodwill for Round 2. I finally unloaded Bree and, with a smile, got back in my car.

But wait! The driver behind me got out of her car.

"What's wrong with that bike?" She asked.

"Nothing, I just don't need it anymore."

"Can I have it?"

The employee stepped up to speak to the woman, "Well technically she already donated it, so you can buy it. But if she says she wants it back, you can both drive outside the entrance and she can give it to you."

So, of course, that's just what we did.

I felt so happy! I was finally giving him to someone who would love him!

Once I loaded it in her Jeep she said, "What a great bike. I can't wait to use the parts!"

And so, thus ended the saga of me trying to do best by Bree. I tried to find the perfect way to part with him, but three hours of time and loads of stress later I wondered, was that worth it?

No.

Things are temporary. Yes, they can be precious, bringing back memories of experiences and people. But they are simply a means to an end. And when our things start owning us, that's when we need to let go.

Goodbye

Joy and I had been friends for nine years, since our sophomore year in high school. We had gotten close fast, and though we only spent two years at the same school, our friendship continued to deepen. We went to youth group together. She did my hair and makeup for prom. We had countless sleepovers and movie nights.

When I left for college, our communication switched from consistent to intermittent. But she always came through. She drove down once a semester to spend time with me. She kept up with what was going in my life and checked in.

But after college, our relationship began to shift. The length of time between text responses began increasing. She began making new, closer friends. When she got engaged, I found out via a Facebook wall post rather than a phone call or text. And I could feel our friendship slowly slipping away.

Sometimes a lighthearted message from me would reel us back to each other and reignite the back-and-forth texts. But eventually, her replies stopped coming. I reached out countless times and got nothing in return for months. After about nine months of unanswered messages, I sent her one that ended like this:

"So the ball is in your court. I would love to hear from you, but the emotional energy it takes from me to keep reaching out and get no reply, or one so late I forgot I sent it, I can't keep up. So when you have your energy back, let me know. You know how to reach me.

Love you."

After weeks of waiting, nothing came back.

But I didn't push it. I left the ball in her court. It was up to her to pick it up.

Months went by and I still hadn't heard a thing, but my wedding was coming up and I wanted her to be there. She was one of my closest friends. So I sent the Save The Date.

Nothing.

I sent the invitation.

Nothing.

I called her, got her voicemail, and left a message.

Nothing.

The wedding date came and went, and no response came.

I waited a few months after the wedding, but the silence only became louder.

So I wrote a final message. I let her go. It seemed so trite to do it on Facebook, but that was the only way I could see if she received it or not. And I knew that she used Facebook. Over the recent months, I'd seen countless pictures of her and her friends on it. Since I hadn't heard from her in so long, I worried that something was seriously wrong. Maybe she was hurt or sick. But judging from her pictures, that didn't seem to be the case.

At the end of the message, I asked her not to respond and blocked her. This was one of the hardest and harshest things I've done. As a people-pleaser, I try not to offend anyone, and yet I had just cut off one of my best friends. But I couldn't do it any longer. My heart couldn't go through the pain of waiting each week for a response, hoping for a relationship reconciliation. Though love had created those bonds, now love allowed me to cut the ties which were not healthy for my heart anymore.

And therein lies the delicate yet determined nature of unbridling oneself from the grip of perfection.

She was my closest friend. If only we could reconnect then we could get back the ideal friendship I'd searched so long for. But it obviously wasn't perfect. And accepting that was another step along the journey to living more fully.

Losing a friend is one of the hardest things to endure. Though the person is still alive, someone has chosen to kill the friendship. In this case, I felt that the relationship was already dead, I was just the one to bury it. And with death comes grief.

This grief is just as hard to bear when you are on the other side as well. The cross country moves aren't so bad, but the voluntary endings cut deep. I've had close relationships broken both through direct verbiage and ghosting. When the messages were conveyed to me, they read like this:

"You're too judgmental,"

"You aren't interesting enough,"

"You are too demanding,"

Basically they were all saying, "You aren't worth my time,"

And while those statements may be true, friends who are meant to be yours will bare those burdens with you.

So if you've had people leave you, leave them behind too. I used to question incessantly, trying to figure out how I could've fixed the friendship. What could I have done differently? What if I had been better? Would my life be more complete with those people in it? Those questions can't be answered and aren't worth your time pouring over again and again. Instead, I'm taking stock of who has stuck around. My parents. My brother. My childhood friends. My friend I met by chance during freshman year of college. My coworkers who I determined to tolerate but ended up loving. My husband.

Those are the people worth your time. Those are the people who deserve your time. Those are the people who chose you, so choose them.

If your circle isn't very big, thank God. If your social media following isn't bursting at the seams, look at the specific people who take the time to double tap and invest back into them. Though many people may leave you, there will be others who stay. So don't miss those people. Even if they aren't the most interesting or engaging. Even if they are difficult or have issues. If they've stayed, they are worth it.

Connections

Since I've recently entered the full-time work force, this is the first time in my life that I've understood the importance of connections. Yes, I needed letters of recommendation for college, grad school, and my first job, but those were all easily acquired through the professors and supervisors I had within the past one-two years. Those connections didn't require a lot of maintenance.

Now, these connections are up to me to maintain. I don't have an academic advisor whom I meet with once a semester to steer me along to the next step. I don't have a plethora of willing and able professors who have a month long recommendation writing season. What seemed guaranteed and easily accessible is now more difficult.

This is also true about our personal relationships.

In college, it wasn't difficult for me to become connected. I joined at least 20 clubs when I first got to campus. Thus, I was never in want of personal connections and they were easy to maintain. We all lived within the same one-two mile radius. We all had countless friends, interests, and activities in common. We all had access to hundreds of free events each week which was practically built-in hang out time.

As some connections graduated and others waned, I also found myself voluntarily pairing down my friendships in search of more quality over quantity. I realized there were some people who I was choosing to spend hours with that I didn't really like. Others were fine to talk to, but we had limited interests in common, and thus little chance for continuing the relationship. And still others I liked, but they wanted to talk and drink for hours when I ached to move and explore.

At countless events, I felt trapped between wanting to share in the camaraderie yet yearning to have people in my life to truly share it with past the current activity.

Being around people is supposed to be intrinsically rewarding. But when you realize it isn't, how do you peel yourself out of a system that you've already ingrained yourself in? How do you start saying no? And how do you not offend those who invited you to show up?

You just do it.

You take the first step and say no. Not because you have plans. Not even because you don't want to go. But because you'd rather invest in something else. Your pottery. The guitar. That book you picked up two months ago. Yourself.

You allow yourself the "luxury" of "selfishness."

Maybe you can't fathom turning down invitations just because you'd rather spend your time differently. Maybe you've been taught that that's rude. Maybe you believe that if someone asks something of you then it must be given. But you only have a limited amount of certain resources. By saying yes to this invitation, you are saying no to spending those hours differently. And if others think they have a right to your time, money, or energy, then they are the selfish ones.

In going to events that you aren't interested in, to be around people that you don't like, what connections are you really making? And which ones are you sacrificing in the process?

Because it's not people at those one-time events or at the bar with whom you create deep friendships. It's the people who are with you in your everyday and routine encounters. It's the people who text the meaningful with the mundane: "How was your meeting today?", "Want to Skype tonight to watch that show?". It's the people who, week by week and month by month, show up so that you truly know them each year.

I searched so long for my ideal friend group. The perfect connections. The people who would keep plans, would enjoy my plethora of activities and interests, would be funny and helpful, and would be enjoyable at any event. I yearned for the people who would stay. That's why I was in so many clubs and spent so much time with people. I was constantly searching. But when I didn't find them, I only drained myself and those around me by continuing my search. And I missed the people in front of me.

Some people may come in and out of your life, and that's ok too. Every year around the holidays, I get together with old college friends. Though we haven't seen each other over the year, we pick up right where we left off. We are still, to some degree, known by each other even without regular intervals of interactions.

Whenever we reconnect I think, "Man, I really want to get together with these people more often! Some of them are only an hour away." But then I go home, settle in, and remind myself that I am trying to do less. Those reconnections are still valuable and I can still be grateful for the time I do get to spend with them, even if those interactions don't translate into more time spent together.

Though time and space may pass between you, there are some people with whom you never lose that connection.

City

Brunches. Baby Showers. Birthdays. Oh my!

Within the span of a week, I find myself invited to a myriad of events. And I'm not counting the Facebook "Events In Your Area" "invitations". I'm talking about the texted, spoken, and emailed invitations. So I've started keeping a list of how many invitations I receive for each day.

Here's this week's:

Monday: 2

Tuesday: 1

Friday: 1

Saturday: 3

How many did I actually want to go to?

Saturday: 1

This list isn't to tote my popularity, but rather to illustrate a point. All but one event involved sitting and eating a meal. For half of the events, I didn't know anyone else going, save the host. Since I like to be physically active and am an introvert, that left only one event that I truly wanted to participate in.

There are so many grabs for our time, and we have to be intentional about not getting pulled to each one. This is true both in professional and personal realms. And it's especially true when you live in a highly populated area.

Living near a city gives you access to a lot of people. When you move to a city, it's easy to connect with people thanks to meet ups and the plethora of activities around. Living near a city for eight years means that you already know said people.

Many of them stayed around after college because jobs were abundant. Others moved back after grad school. Those who you knew from different times and places may move to your city as well. Today, I have people around me who I've known since childhood along with those I met last week.

While having this amount of known people available is comforting to some, to others it seems like there aren't enough hours in the day for everyone. Well, that's because there aren't. For people you've known for a few years, you go through the cycle of dinner catch ups. For those you've just met, you go out for coffee or drinks for some get-to-know-you sessions. For those who've recently moved from your original hometown, you meet each other's significant others, babies, and dogs. And by the end of that, it's time to start all over again.

Not only is that exhausting, but while you are doing all of this, what is the end goal? To keep up with everyone just in time to restart the cycle? To keep yourself busy to stave off loneliness? To have stories to tell when someone asks, "What did you do last night?" By keeping on the periphery of everyone's lives you leave no time to dive deeply into anyones. And that's the real crisis.

Once entrenched in this cycle, you may not even realize who you like hanging out with and who you are just around. Sometimes, when I look at my calendar for the week, I find that I don't have one evening free. And I didn't plan any of the outings.

If you find yourself dissatisfied with this pattern, then ask yourself, "Do I even want to be with these people, or am I just accepting invitations because that's the socially obligatory thing to do?" Just because you are "free" that night, doesn't mean that your only option is to pile on something else to do.

Another issue with living near a city is the transitory nature of those who live there. Many people move to a city with a short-term goal in mind. My close proximity to Washington D.C brings lots of two-year assignment military personnel into the area. Others come looking for a "fresh start" or a new city to explore until the next round of wanderlust sets in. While it's a great situation for those who want to "meet people", it's terrible for building lasting relationships. Yes, I can keep up with everyone on social media, but in terms of deep connections, that's more difficult. And so, you are left with a large amount of people around you who's only guarantee is that they won't be staying long.

Since I've had almost a decade in this area to make these small connections, I find myself inundated with an endless amount of invitations from people all over the spectrum of known-ness and longevity. When such a large amount of people are crammed into one space, it's easy to go down the Facebook friends list, invite everyone within a couple square miles, and have a packed party. But there is a difference between being wanted at an event and the invitee being fine with your presence there. There is a big difference between someone texting you, "Hope you can make it!" and a mass notification sent out to the other 200 people invited. And the difference can have a substantial impact on your physical, emotional, and mental well-being.

If someone wants you at an event and individually tells me so, I am at least 50% more likely to attend and 100% more likely to enjoy myself. If someone mass-invites you just to have a noteworthy amount of people at their event, you will likely spend at least some amount of time wishing to get out of conversations, wishing to be doing something else, and/or wishing to be home. Is that any way to spend any amount of your time? You are only given a finite amount of it. If you are likely not to enjoy yourself, bet on those odds and decline. If they really wanted you there, they would say so. And then, odds are, you might actually be glad you came.

Maybe you have the opposite problem. Maybe you're thinking, "I don't have enough people in my life and I want more. I don't have endless possibilities of connections to choose from and wish I did." I bet you do.

First, use who you already have in your life. Invest deeper into the people you consider your close friends. Try a hobby they like or spend the better part of a day together. Next, think about those on the periphery that you'd like to draw in closer and make it happen. Who was the last person you had an unexpectedly pleasant interaction with? Whose social media picture did you recently double tap? Send a text or make a call. Chances are you have more people around you who you could make substantial connections with than you realize.

After this, if you feel that you still need an outlet, go online. Find a meet-up or go volunteer. Go to an event or activity that's interesting to you and talk to the people there, even if it's just one conversation with one person. It may take some time before something sticks or you find a kindred spirit, but it will happen. Most people around you are looking for connection too.

Sometimes we have to go outside of ourselves to find something lasting. Valuable people and relationships aren't easy to come by, and that's what makes them worth it. There are no perfect relationships, but all of them can be rewarding.

As Jonathan Van Ness says on his podcast "Getting Curious", "I always find something that I'm obsessed with about someone." And I'm sure you can too.

Delete

Going through any social media can be both exhilarating and exhausting. You find out which of your high school friends got married. You get a sneak-peek into the lives of your favorite sports/music/movie stars. Maybe you even get a follow-back or a re-tweet. But you also end up wasting a lot of time collecting details of lives that you have no place in. You gather facts about others' lives instead of living your own. And once you know these meaningless facts about people who don't have any impact on your real life, you've also wasted time you could've spent with people in your 3D life.

And then there's the other side of the coin—the part where you interact with all of your followers. Instead of a voice-to-voice interaction where you tell someone something and they respond, you may say something and get nothing in response. You have no idea how many people saw it, which ones read it, smiled at it, shed a tear, scrolled without noticing, or cared at all. And even if the results are more negative than positive, wouldn't knowing be better than not?

I am not the only person I know who does a "purge" of people on my social media. While it can seem harsh or unnecessarily mean, it's freeing. And that freedom—of your time, your emotional energy, your mental carriage—that's more important than worrying about the feelings of someone who you don't interact with and will never see again.

Deleting isn't only for followers, but also for social media platforms as a whole. Every time you post a picture on Instagram, how many of you also hit the button to post it to Facebook? I know I did. Why? I wanted everyone to see it. I wanted as many likes and notifications as possible for the maximum dopamine hit. But then, I noticed that both of my feeds were filled with the same pictures over and over because all my friends were doing the exact same thing. And scrolling through the same 20 photos for the first minute is terribly unenjoyable. So why was I doing it too?

I decided to primarily use one social media platform. So which did I choose? I like photography and want to get better at it so I decided to use Instagram. I hope this will set an intention when I use social media so that I see more of what I want and less of what I don't. Even if I miss some Facebook-suggested-cute-shelter-dogs-get-rescued video that I cry at every time. If it was really important to me to watch those, there are hours of YouTube videos I could intentionally find. And then I'm taking ownership of what I consume instead of just letting it happen to me. I am taking control of my content, and you should too.

Using social media for hours is also tied to people's perceptions of us. This is true for the people on the other side of the screen, and the people on the other side of the aisle. Look around you when you are commuting, sitting in a doctor's office, or waiting in line at the check out. Oh wait, you can't, because you are on your phone too!

Why is it more socially appropriate to be staring at your phone rather than staring at the wall? Both usually garner the same result. But looking at your phone is more socially acceptable because it shows other people that you are busy. It looks like you are either important or getting things done, neither of which have to be true. You could just be looking at cat memes. But when we look like we aren't popular or constantly doing something, we are seen as less. In trying to gain more (social media presence, likes, followers, knowledge, power), we get less (time, energy, real relationships, money, rest). When you fill up your time to the max, you are left with little in return.

We spend so many of our waking hours crafting perfection on social media too. We take a "totally candid, but 100% meant for Instragram" photo, use a filter, think of an eye-catching, thought-provoking, or like-producing caption, hashtag it with witty phrases, and send it off to the world with an attitude of "my life is better than yours." We try to get a certain number of followers and likes, and if we don't, then it truly affects us. We feel shamed. All because our lives aren't as "liked" as we'd like them to be. Or because our friends pictures routinely get 100 likes while ours only net 20. And instead of thinking, "What's wrong with this cycle?" we think, "What's wrong with my life?" Seeking perfection often steals more than it rewards.

We ascribe so much value to the popular rather than the people whom we love and live life with. We post pictures of us with famous faces rather than the ones who are individually famous to us. We celebrate the accomplishments of people who will never know our names, let alone any significant detail about our life. We want a certain number of likes rather than likes from certain people. And this sad cycle causes us to miss the people in front of us. The ones who actually care about us, and who we should actually care about too.

At the end of the day, here's the real question when it comes to social media: Why do we spend so much time worrying about what other's think? Maybe it's because we interact with some of these people on an ongoing basis and their opinion of us impacts facets of our lives. But for those whom we don't and never again will share face time, their opinions truly don't matter. And once we accept that truth, we have more time and space for those who do matter.

Wedding

It wasn't supposed to rain. Yes, we had set the date for April, but it wouldn't rain. We were getting married outside. We had the arch and the flowers. We chose a spot on the water. I was wearing white. So it couldn't rain.

Friday was gorgeous: 70 and sunny. While the weather apps showed storm clouds for Saturday, I willed them away. Sunday was also bright and glorious; unseasonably warm weather for April. It was almost as if something had to be sacrificed for the sake of these two perfect days.

And that sacrifice was our wedding day.

My bridesmaids and I got to the venue at 9:00am. It was already nasty out. The rain was spitting on and off and the landscape was gray with haze. The ceremony was at 4:45pm. Plenty of time for it to clear up! It couldn't stay like this all day, right?

Oh, yes it could. And it did.

In the morning, the event coordinators came up to our getting ready room to let us know the plan.

"Ok, so we will move the ceremony to the tent instead of outside. We can move the reception tables to the side, then back to the center after the ceremony. We'll get out the umbrellas for you girls to use when you walk from the house to the tent. This happens all the time. We will work it out."

And just like that, my dream was dead. I didn't even get a say. I couldn't even get a question in before they were back down the stairs, making the preparations to tear apart a big piece of the day I'd planned for nine months, and a few years of my single life as well.

Most people would take this in stride, or at least not see this as big a deal as I did. Others may have thought, "Oh well, something is bound to go wrong today, right?" But not this. This is the one thing that could not go wrong.

I hid the tears until I could excuse myself downstairs. We were getting ready in the house on the property, so there were plenty of unused rooms. I found one in the back, closed the door, and wept.

I wept for my plans. I wept for my vision. I wept for my photos. I wept for my little girl dreams.

Why did this matter to me so much? Because I love the outdoors. Because my nickname in college was Sunny. Because nature has healed me in more ways than one.

But like anything important, I elevated it to a point of no return. Since I couldn't achieve my dreams based on factors I couldn't control, I was left with a weight of disappointment much too great to carry. Let alone on this day.

There were other disappointments too. We didn't have enough time for pictures. We didn't have enough time to greet everyone. We had to hurry the DJ along. We had to leave the venue much earlier than we were ready to.

But there were equally as many joys. We still took great pictures. We got a beautiful sunset. We talked to, laughed with, and danced alongside all our friends. We had an amazing after-party.

Thankfully, I didn't miss these beautiful moments. But if I wasn't so focused on my definition of perfection in the first place, I probably would've noticed more.

Why do we spend so much time crafting perfection? Nothing in this world is perfect. Don't we know that? So we should just be able to let it go, right?

I believe we yearn for perfection because we were made for it. It's why athletes train for the Olympics. It's why artists spend years curating their piece. It's why physicians are in school for at least eight years before treating a patient on their own. We are constantly on this quest to find perfect because our hearts are restless for it.

The search for perfection starts from a good place. Who doesn't like the Olympics? Wouldn't the "Mona Lisa" be less striking without the decades behind it? Who wants a doctor who hasn't perfected their practice?

But if we seek perfection endlessly, we tend to be dissatisfied with what's in front of us, with what we've already accomplished. It's why people go to the gym six times a week. It's why we are on social media for over two hours a day. [4] It's why people sink into deep, dark hurt and aren't able to climb out.

So I'm posing two things:

    1. Perfection isn't possible

    2. We should seek out "better" rather than perfect, and find joy in that instead.

When you want something to be perfect and it's not, think of all the baby steps you've taken to get where you are. Remember all the progress you've already achieved, instead of being weighed down by the setbacks. A lot of times, seeking perfection can hold us back from doing anything at all.

When you measure your progress, don't use others as a relative mark, use yourself. Instead of asking, "Am I as fit as that cross-fit model?" ask, "Can I do more sit ups than a week ago?" Instead of asking, "Will I publish as many book as J.K Rowling?" ask, "Did I write more pages than yesterday?" Instead of asking, "Could I ever be as rich as Kim Kardashian?" ask, "Am I making more financially smart decisions than I was last year?"

By looking at your own life as a measuring stick, you can count your victories as they come, not as they relate to others. Another reason you can't compare yourself to others is that you don't have the life they do! You don't have the time to work out for hours a day. You don't have the mind to imagine Harry Potter and all of his outstanding adventures. You don't have the financial leg up to rise to fortune as quickly. So don't look so much at other's lives—look at your own.

And that's what I should've done. Instead of comparing my wedding to an Instagram post with 5,000 likes, I should've looked at my own. Was there natural beauty around me? Was there a barn? Were the decorations just right? Were the centerpieces exactly what I pictured? Were the people I loved around me? A resounding yes to all. And by focusing on that, I'm sure the only tears to shed would've been happy ones.

Solo

"If you're seeking perfection, free soloing is as close as you can get,"

-Alex Honnold in the film "Free Solo".

Watching this movie brought up a lot more emotion in me than I expected. Though I've loved climbing for the past six years, it hasn't been my priority lately. This movie made me remember.

When I was young, I thought that the ultimate height of coolness was outdoor rock climbing. I guess I'd seen people do it on TV, because we didn't live anywhere near the mountains. The first time I tried to climb a rock wall I was at a retreat center with my family. The employee got me harnessed up and I was so excited; I had wanted to do this for years! Then he asked how old I was.

"Twelve,"

You had to be thirteen. I was devastated.

I think my dad got me ice-cream instead, which solved the crisis for the time being. But my need to climb wasn't fully realized until I started chasing it.

When I got to college, I started exploring the paths I longed to trek in high school, such as climbing. And The University of Maryland happened to have an outdoor climbing wall.

My first time at the wall, I went casually with friends. It was a ton of fun. The people there were super cool, like I always thought. I was finally over the age limit! Afterwards, muscles I never knew I had ached. And I knew I wanted to feel like that everyday.

So I kept going.

And going.

And going.

Until one day I was that cool person. I was climbing everyday. I was going on weekend trips with friends. I was camping and climbing during yearly pilgrimages to The New River Gorge in West Virginia. I was learning how to lead climb outdoors. I was having the time of my life.

And until I watched "Free Solo", I didn't fully know why.

Though I'd never climb at the level of Alex, who routinely climbs thousands of feet without ropes, I identify a lot with him when I think back to my beginning days of climbing. When I climbed, I felt free. When I climbed, I felt at peace. When I climbed, I felt whole.

Now I am out of practice and only climb a few times a year. Now I feel a lot differently. I feel fear. I feel the eyes of others. I feel trapped in the space between what I used to do and now can't.

But I realized that I identify with Alex for another reason as well: the power of being in the present. When I climb, I don't think about anything but climbing. When I climb, there is no past or future. When I climb, I'm not thinking my normal streams of multiple thoughts at once. When I climb, I'm not worrying about my presentation the next day or the meetings I had last week. Climbing is as much a mental game as it is a physical one. Maybe even more so the former than the latter. And you have to be present for it.

To some extent, I wish I could do it solo. I get so tired of waiting on others, on having to find people to go climbing with, and the limitations of the gear I don't have and the places I long to go. When I have a desire to do something—like climb— sometimes it seems to connect with my soul with such an urgency that it must be done NOW or never. And my perfectionism makes me think the later is more likely.

This can be unbearably frustrating, as this state of waiting can feel so constant, and sometimes I feel ready to burst. I feel that, by keeping dreams and hopes locked away, they get repressed, and either I lash out in resentment or the dreams simply die.

But this waiting also keeps the dreams alive. It reminds me that there is still plenty of time left to accomplish them. And I've learned that it's also ok if those dreams change into something else entirely.

We are all born with desires and dreams. We all ache for the world to function in a certain way, and that's not bad. But it's also not possible a lot of the time. And accepting that frees you more than summiting all the mountains and climbing all the pitches ever will.

Yes, free soloing requires perfection, and some choose this avenue to achieve it. But one consequence of that is death. And if that is the cost of perfection, then we don't all need to aim for that.

"If I find in myself a desire in which no experience in this world can satisfy, the most probable explanation is that I was made for another world."

-C.S Lewis in his book, "Mere Christianity" [5]

Place

I awoke to the early morning rays through the window of the cab. I knew the alarm was going to go off any minute so I rolled over, wishing for a few extra minutes of some semblance of sleep. We had slept in the back of the truck for three days and three nights, during which time I'd tried and failed to find comfort in every sleeping position possible.

When the alarm went off, I knew what time it was: 6:00am. We'd agreed to meet at 6:30am. Now it was time to climb out of the truck bed, walk to the bathroom in the cold, and get ready for the very thing I was dreading.

This wasn't boot camp; this was vacation.

When we arrived at the site, it was 6:20am. I can't remember if we had breakfast or not. If we did, it was oatmeal out of the packet because we didn't have any bowls. We also shared spoons, which still had residue from the last time they were used.

At 6:30am on the dot, our fourth partner pulled up. Still not believing this was happening, I suited up with my gear and we started walking to the crag. I was shaking with fear.

I told myself many things that morning, going back and forth between my two options:

A: "You don't have to do this,"

B: "This is the reason we drove the extra eight hours here—of course you have to!"

A: "If you don't feel comfortable, say no,"

B: "You will never have this opportunity again!"

A: "You're not ready for this,"

B: "You've been training for years for this!"

Once we got to the crag, it was time to put on our harnesses and shoes. During this time, I decided I was going to do this. I didn't have to like it, but I was doing it.

Adam and our fourth man, Dave, went first. Dave was our Canadian rock climbing guide whom we'd met by chance the day before. When we explained to him that we were doing this route, he asked if he could come with us. Then he mentioned that he was training to be a rock climbing guide and would love the practice. His girlfriend begged us to say yes. Otherwise, he was going to do some free soloing. We happily obliged.

When it came for Noah's and my turn, he asked me, "Are you nervous?"

"Well, it would help if I knew what I was doing," I replied.

"Oh, right," he laughed.

He explained how we would clip in, how to give slack, and how many pitches we would go up. While I knew most of the instructions, the last time I climbed on real rock was years ago. The last time I multi-pitch climbed on real rock was never.

We were sport climbing. This is a type of rock climbing where someone has previously gone up and bolted in rings for you to clip your rope into as you climb. I had done this countless times, both at the gym and outdoors. But I hadn't done this up a 1,000 foot rock face. Since I live on the east coast, most of the accessible climbing isn't very tall. Thus, once you climb about seven bolts, you are at the top.

Today's climbing was different. Today, Noah would go up seven bolts and clip himself into the bolt. Then, he would belay me from above, off the side of the mountain —up those same seven bolts to where he was. Once I got there, I would clip into the bolt. Noah would attach himself back into the rope and climb the next seven bolts and I would belay him, from the side of the mountain. We would do this over and over again, until we either reached the top or got too tired or scared. I knew the latter would occur way before the former ever would.

While climbing the fourth pitch, I was wrecked. I was terrified and had Elvis-legs (that feeling you get while climbing when your legs shake uncontrollably). I was talking to myself—sometimes comforting, sometimes belittling, sometimes ordering to get through it. But mostly, I was crying.

Because we kept missing bolts, one pitch turned into two. Thus, on top of the fifth pitch, I finally tapped out. It was a good place to do so because there was a view. That also meant there was more scope of just how far off the ground we were. I don't consider myself scared of heights, but strapped into the side of a mountain that day, I was. Oh, and did I mention that it was snowing?

We all got down in one piece. Back at the car, we were elated. At one point in my climbing life, this was my dream. While I set it aside during graduate school and working, it still felt surreal that I had accomplished it. And while I won't be doing it again soon, I'm glad I did it.

At the bottom, we decided on a place to get burgers and beers. This was our last day in Canada, and after lunch we were set to drive back over the border to Montana where a room, shower, and bed awaited us.

Once on the road, we had just started our four hour drive. It was my turn to drive and Noah was helping me choose songs for my American Idol Audition. We were cruising for about 40 minutes. I had to keep remembering to look at the red kilometer numbers rather than the black mile ones to determine my speed.

Then the standstill traffic jam hit. We later learned the cause; a fatality during an accident had shut down the one major highway we needed to take. Thus, we could not make it through—we had to go around the highway. Luckily, we were one of the first cars that the traffic cop diverted, so we rolled down the windows to ask for directions. Since we hadn't bought SIM cards, our cell phones didn't work and all we had were paper maps. Thankfully, the cop's directions led us to the paralleling highway. We were cruising again! For about 20 minutes. Then we were stuck in the same traffic that had also been diverted from the highway. Except, instead of four lanes, this "highway" had one lane. So this was going to take awhile.

At the time, we had no way of knowing how long it would last. We had no GPS to show us the red traffic line. We had no ETA. We had no knowledge of the area and no clue how far out the way this new route was taking us. But we did know one thing: we had nine hours until the border closed and we were not spending another night in the back of this truck.

So first we were in Denial: "This can't last that long. We will come to the end of it soon."

This soon turned to Anger: "This is taking so long! I can't believe this is happening to us!"

Which morphed into Bargaining: "If we can just get to a point where we are constantly moving, then it'll be ok."

Then Depression: "We are never going to get out of this. We are going to be stuck in this so long that we will miss the 10:00pm border closing and will have to spend another night in the back of this truck."

Then, finally, Acceptance: "We are stuck in this truck and will deal with the consequences, whatever they may be."

Yes, we went through the 5 Stages of Grief during the ride.

Our new detour was also taking us through farm country, and you know what they don't have? Public restrooms. Since I am not a male, it's not as easy for me to pull off the side of the highway, but that's exactly what we had to do. I won't go into the details, but they included towels and kids laughing at us out of their car windows as the line of traffic inched by us.

Yes, this was still our vacation: the thing we save up our time and money all year for to voluntarily go enjoy. We had already gotten up before the sun to conquer a fear in the snow, and now we were wasting the rest of the day sitting in the car.

And so, what did I do? I worried. I worried about not crossing the border in time. I worried about not having a bed to sleep in. I worried so much and for so long that I gave myself continuous headaches throughout the journey. In fact, I was unconsciously clenching my jaw so hard that when I eventually tried to eat something, I couldn't.

While all my fears and anxieties were swirling around my head, I almost missed the beauty around me. The rolling Canadian hills. The interplay between sun and darkening clouds that can be seen for miles with no obstructions. The multiple rainbows. The foals jumping and chasing their tails in the fields. And the conversation around me.

When we got to the hotel, we would be doing the same thing: sitting around talking—we were too tired to do anything else— so why was I so mad that we were doing the same thing in the car? Because it wasn't perfect. Because we were crammed into a small space for much longer than we planned. Because there were so many things that could go wrong if we didn't make it in time.

But we did make it in time—eight hours later, but still one hour before the border closed for the evening. That night, we each had a bed to sleep in and we were warm for the first time in three days. Everything worked out. In the end, my worries did me no good.

And in the end, I learned three things:

1. We should look at obstacles as opportunities. While life is more bearable when it's easy, it's not worth much. If you never have to struggle for anything, you will never know the valuable from the worthless.

2. We should choose to see challenges as chances. This is a chance for you to continue learning to be calm in the face of anxiety. This is a chance for you to continue saying no even when you're socially pressured. This is a chance for you to keep taking steps down

the path to your better life by letting go of

expectations of yourself and others and just

breathe.

3. We should spend more time enjoying the

present. Wherever you are, be there.

FOMO

I don't need to write that one out, do I? So many people use this acronym to replace the words in it that **FOMO** was added to the Oxford English Dictionary in 2013. If you need a more exact description, here's one: "...the uneasy and sometimes all-consuming feeling that you're missing out – that your peers are doing, in the know about, or in possession of more or something better than you". [6]

An article in "Time" completes this definition with some more concrete ways that **FOMO** manifests itself:

"It's certainly not a good thing. And it leads you to check social media again and again and again so you don't feel out of the loop. So you know you're doing okay. So you don't feel left out.

Sometimes that alleviates the anxiety — but often it doesn't. And either way it drives you to keep running around the digital hamster wheel to feel okay with yourself....

Um, sounds uncomfortably like addiction to me..." [7]

Further research has concluded: "The problem with FOMO is the individuals it impacts are looking outward instead of inward," McLaughlin said. "When you're so tuned in to the 'other,' or the 'better' (in your mind), you lose your authentic sense of self. This constant fear of missing out means you are not participating as a real person in your own world." [8]

While a lot of FOMO is linked to social media usage and consumption, not all of it is. FOMO is the reason that we allow people to stay over past their welcome. It's the reason we go camping for the 15th time even though we figured out we hated it by the 3rd. It's the reason we accept every invitation to every event in the off-chance that this one will be different than the others. And it's the reason we are so unhappy and depressed.

One study found specifically which negative results were associated with FOMO. "It was also associated with the predicted negative outcomes, such as fatigue, stress, sleep problems, and psychosomatic symptoms." [9]

How many of you could have also predicted at least one of those words in that thread? Yet, we still allow ourselves to get caught up in a cycle that we know is detrimental.

My FOMO manifests itself a bit differently. Because I am a planner, I try to combat FOMO by filling up my time with all the experiences I can hold, and then some. That way, if I do find myself jealous of others for their experiences I can say, "Well, at least I've had mine."

It's as if I think the only way to do life right is through One Republic's song, "I Lived"

> "I did it all
>
> I owned every second
>
> that this world could give
>
> I saw so many places, the things that I did
>
> Yeah with every broken bone
>
> I swear I lived."

While these words inspire some to accomplish their dreams, this way of thinking actually further compounds my anxiety. It means, no matter how much I've done, I will never feel as if I've "done it all". It means that every wedding invitation turns into a weekend getaway. It means that every Winter, Spring, and Summer break turn into a trip because, "This may be the last time I can do this." And when I don't get to have those experiences, I feel as if I've wasted the time. So that when FOMO comes around, I have less to combat it with.

What if I lived by Johnny Diaz's song, "Just Breathe", instead?

"Just breathe (just breathe)

Let your weary spirit rest

Lay down what's good and find what's best

Just breathe (just breathe)."

Don't ever think this is your last or only chance. You don't know that. And living as if it is will just leave you searching for the next chance. Don't spend your life in constant search of more—it will never end.

When you find out what you actually like and want to do rather than just what you've been tolerating, you can let go of FOMO. You don't have to wish you were at every event, experiencing everything, because you know what you truly want to spend your time doing. Say yes to those opportunities instead.

My most recent case of FOMO: The Capitols won the NHL Stanley Cup for the first time in history and the players were partying all over Washington D.C. My friends and I spent hours sending each other messages about their Instagram stories. First, they were at the Nationals Baseball game doing keg stands on the Stanley Cup. Then, they were spotted walking down the streets with it. Finally, they went to the Georgetown Waterfront for a swim in the fountains.

At some point I thought, "I could go join in the fun. I'm only an hour metro ride away. I could go on a wild goose chase with my friends to find them!" But when I got there, was I really going to experience a greater amount of joy than I was currently? Probably not. I believe I was getting 10 times more joy watching the videos from my couch and laughing with my husband than I ever would have in D.C on a quest to quell my FOMO.

When did FOMO become the law instead of our own internal compasses? And if I believe that my greatest commodity is my time, why aren't I taking more control of it?

Don't try to fill up your time with all of the perfect experiences, places, and people. They don't exist. Instead, accept and revel in what and who's around you already. Take time to enjoy rather than just consume.

There are some views I will never see. But in chasing after all of them, I miss the ones in front of me.

Create

Recently, after coming back from our third weekend vacation this year (not counting our 10 day trip to Montana and Canada), my husband made a good observation: when I plan the vacations, we come back more tired than when we left. Why? Because I want to do all the things. I want to accomplish so much, and that means we don't actually get to rest.

On said trip to Montana, we hiked over 70 miles in 7 days. Up mountains. In high altitudes. In the cold. With no training. By the middle of our trip, we were exhausted. One day we drove to our hiking spot, only to fall asleep in the truck bed. Then, we went into the adjacent lodge and spent the afternoon sitting in the lounge, drinking hot chocolate, and just resting. By the final two days, we were spending the majority of the time in the lodge, watching World Cup Soccer, and getting up just to eat and stretch our legs.

Where was the vacation? Yes, it was tons of fun, but we also did way too much and consequently were burned out by the time we were supposed to feel refreshed.

One reason this happens is because I feel the weight of the competition to have the best vacation ever, and that comes with stories. Who wants to hear about how many hours you slept or how many margaritas you had at the pool? You could do that anywhere!

But can you?

The point is, when you are on vacation you are away from your obligations. You literally have no one to see and nothing to get done. So why do we create things to accomplish? Do we want to measure up to others? Do we want to seize the day? Do we want to do all the things in this location so we can then go chase all the other places on our bucket lists? Do we think we will find perfection in these places and experiences?

We spend so much time doing and not enough time being. Being still. Being hopeful. Being grateful. Being calm. Being present. We need more time to just exist. Because it's in this time—in these spaces provided when we don't fill them up—that we find what we want to create. We find what we enjoy and want more of. We find what we can get rid of and live without. We find what makes us whole and how to take more steps toward that end.

But finding that space and time to just be isn't going to be easy. Why? Because our culture tells us that's not what's important. In fact, our culture tells us that's wasteful, and maybe even selfish. But our culture also tells us to consume and do more so that we can be filled up with as much as possible. Unfortunately, the result of this "fill up" is just more emptiness if you aren't intentional with how you are spending your resources.

And so, you have to create that time for yourself.

I want to create and not just consume.

"Life has a temple we never have time for

Feels like we're all missing out

No time for the beauty that always surrounds me

Walking with my head hanging down...

I'm running, my eyes closed, I'm running

I try to keep up with all those around me

I find that I'm rushing, I can't see

All of the beautiful things until you make the world stand still

You make me see and feel

I keep spinning around until you slow me down

You make me real

When you make the world stand still"

-"World Stand Still" by The Tenors

Slow

I don't have time for the unexpected. So when it inevitably happens, my response is pure annoyance. Like when my work had a potluck on Friday, but I didn't hear about it until the Tuesday before.

"But I already went to the grocery store for this week!" I complained to my coworkers.

They laughed it off as me being sarcastic.

"You're too rigid—you have to be flexible!" One of my friends playfully chided, reciting the vocabulary we often use with our students.

But I was more than half serious. At that point, my weeks were so packed that going to the grocery store for a second trip simply wasn't viable. Well, it was, but that meant shifting a handful of other items with it. And I just wasn't willing to do that.

After these countless instances of trying to fit in as much as possible only to have my plans thwarted, I decided that I needed to scale back. I needed to slow down. This means not only putting less on my calendar, but also physically slowing down my pace.

I'm a fast walker. I can squeeze through crowds with ease. I plan my route around each person, as if they were merely obstacles in a course. I'm used to hearing people startle in surprise as I sneak by them within the aisles of the supermarket. When I'm hiking, I count how many people I pass along the way. I'm accustomed to friends running to catch up with me if we are walking a distance greater than 500 feet.

I realized that even when I'm walking within my building I act like I'm training for the Olympic power-walking team. So now, I'm reminding myself to s-l-o-w d-o-w-n. Before I make a movement, I try to take at least one calming, meditative breath, even if I'm just moving room-to-room. It's amazing how much of a difference a simple intention can make.

Trying to get places fast is me seeking efficiency. If I get somewhere quicker, I can get to more places in the same amount of time, right? And that means I can get more done. But this isn't necessarily true. If I have too much quantity (ie. places traveled), I am definitely sacrificing quality (ie. time spent in those places).

Why do delicious restaurants get their stellar reviews and long wait lists? Conversely, why is it easy to pick up a meal from McDonald's? Quality matters. And it takes time to produce.

It's the same with your time. If you are dealing it out to everyone, cutting it up into tiny chunks here and there trying to get as much done as possible, you won't produce quality of any sort. You won't be able to analyze what you're doing because you won't be able to remember or synthesize the information. We need to learn to do less by slowing down to create a better result.

So if you find yourself multitasking, stop. Just stop. It doesn't work. Even while we are doing it, we feel that truth. We feel disjointed, moving from one task to another, not able to keep track of where we are in any of them.

"The neuroscience is clear: We are wired to be mono-taskers. One study found that just 2.5% of people are able to multitask effectively. And when the rest of us attempt to do two complex activities simultaneously, it is simply an illusion." [10]

When you get interrupted from a task—whether self-induced or via another person—it takes an average of 23 minutes and 15 seconds to get back to the first task. [11]

Additionally, if we do try to multitask, by the time we are finished, would we be able to replicate what we've done to save time on future, similar tasks? No. Likely we'll be doing more work trying to fix mistakes we made while we were multitasking, while we are in the process of a new project, and that's how the cycle keeps replicating.

When you slow down and stop multitasking, you might notice another component to living in unperfection: quiet. There's a reason that "peace" and "quiet" go together.

Recently I was getting my car's oil changed. The auto shop had a small lounge, so I went into it to escape the heat. I'd brought my book for such an occasion.

When I walked in, I was pleasantly surprised to see I was the only one there. So I got comfortable, brewed some coffee, turned off the TV, and turned down the blasting AC.

After about an hour, an employee walked in. We exchanged polite smiles as she went to throw something in the trash. As she approached, she looked up at the nearby TV.

"Oh!" She said, "The TV got turned off".

I said, "Yeah, I turned it off."

"Oh," She said, looking mildly confused as she walked away.

Are we so accustomed to constant noise that silence seems odd?

Everywhere we go there is noise. Even once we come in off the busy street into a store or an office, the noise continues. Why is there music playing in every store or office? The grocery store. The eye doctor's office. The restaurant. What is the point? You go to these places for a reason that actually requires thought and silence: to pick up what you came for, to understand your diagnosis and plan going forward, to converse and reconnect with a loved one. But somehow, we are conditioned to believe that there isn't value in quiet, and so we must fill up all the space with noise. Why?

People equate silence with sadness or distance. If you are around others and you aren't speaking, people may ask, "Why are you so quiet?", as if it's a bad thing. While this is sometimes true, it's also true that constant talking and noise are often the result of someone's stress and anxiety bubbling over. Maybe, instead of projecting our ideas onto someone else, we should recognize that for some people, being quiet is calming and rebalancing. Let's stop trying to fit everyone inside our boxes of understanding.

Perhaps we also think that silence breeds unproductivity. Yet, I find the opposite to be true.

When I slowed down at work, I produced more quality output. I turned off the fluorescent lights that gave me migraines in return for the gentle glow of a reading lamp. I kept the essential oil diffuser on all day. I set my kids goals in front of me during the session so I can remember the exact wording, cueing provided, and percentage we are aiming for. Both so I can compare their performance to last time and so I can make sure we are hitting the mark this time.

And you know what? My therapy is getting better. I actually know in the moment how my kids are doing. I know how we are doing. I know if I need to tweak my support and exactly how. I analyze and synthesize. And the result? My kids are flourishing. They are shining. Brighter than those fluorescent bulbs ever did.

When we slow down, breathe, and turn off the noise, we may not be missing anything. In fact, we may be gaining a piece of ourselves.

Less

The language we use isn't simple. Unless you're an English teacher, have you ever had to explain to someone how to make verbs past tense? My explanation went like this:

"For most verbs, you add an -ed to the end. Like want becomes wanted. For other verbs, you change the vowel in the middle. Like run becomes ran. But then, for other verbs, there isn't a rule and you just have to memorize it. Like go becomes went."

Have you ever had to explain idioms to someone? How do you explain "coming out of the woodwork" or "icing on the cake"? Some of our figurative language comes from actual experiences which turned into the phrases we know today, but most times, that connection gets lost.

Maybe if we took more time to look more closely at what we are actually saying, our words would matter more. As of now, there are so many words flying around all the time, we can't keep up with them, much less sift through the important from the trivial.

My current role as a Speech-Language Pathologist allows me the privilege of interacting with an amazing group of middle schoolers. As this is only my third year practicing, I am constantly aware of how much growth there is to do. It is so easy to get overwhelmed by all the trainings and programs I want to be versed in someday. But, I've realized that a lot of what my kids need is simplification.

Language is hard for all of my kids. For a myriad of reasons, they did not acquire it as simply as their typically developing peers. And in order to learn it, they need simple.

Sometimes, that means writing a checklist of how to get ready for class.

1. Sit down

2. Put your binder on your desk

3. Open your binder

4. Take out your notes

5. Take out your pencil

Sometimes, that means writing a Venn Diagram of how words are similar and different.

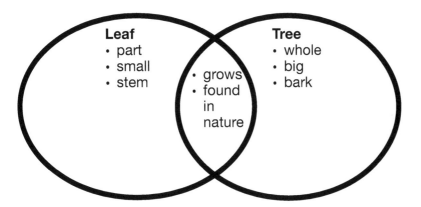

Sometimes, that means making a chart of how to say verbs in the present, past, and future tense.

Past	Present	Future
ran	run, is running	will run
sat	sit, is sitting	will sit
jumped	jump, is jumping	will jump

Whatever the solution, "less is more" has never been more true. This year, I found myself purging a lot of materials, whether I used them or not. I started taking some visuals off of the wall to help my kids focus on the current task. I started to slow down my speaking pace and ramp up my intentionality.

When I first started practicing speech therapy, I thought having the perfect session meant providing different activities for each kid for every session. But it doesn't. That's a lot of unnecessary planning, and it may actually have the opposite effect. First of all, many of my kids have very similar goals. Secondly, I have less planning time than therapy time. And third, success comes from repetition.

When you practice a sport, don't you do the same thing over and over again until you master it? What would happen if you tried a new skill or technique for each session? I bet that you would get marginally good at a lot of skills but you wouldn't master anything. And the same is true with therapy.

Once I started realizing repetition is key, I started using the same materials multiple times with multiple kids. I found which ones worked well and which ones did not. I started pruning my materials to include only the best, instead of all of the potential candidates. My office became more organized, and I became less stressed.

By negating all of the extra time and energy worrying about making a session "new and exciting", I started to see more growth, both in me and the kids. I knew where everything was. I wasn't always fumbling for page numbers and leafing through countless files. I had a vision for what I was doing, where it was located, and how it would best help my kids achieve their goals. My therapy got better because I made it simpler.

At the end of this process, I also found that I had more; more time to actually measure progress instead of trying so hard to produce it. More time to research best practice methods and techniques. More time to get to know my kids and their families, and make an impact past the current objective.

So many times, we think that "working hard" means being constantly busy, reinventing the wheel, and not having a moment to spare. But, in doing so, we miss so much. We miss the funny things our clients say that make the day so enjoyable. We miss the opportunities for short conversations with coworkers that bloom into friendships. Ultimately, we miss the chance to be better people and better professionals because we are too caught up in details that really don't matter.

If I was restricted to only three things to do effective speech therapy with, this would be my list:

1. Whiteboard

2. Dry Erase Marker

3. Eraser

It's just that simple.

When it comes to making progress in both speech therapy and life, do less and you will get more.

Work

With books like, "The 4-Hour Workweek" by Tim Ferriss, you might wonder if the eight hour workday is coming to a close. But when you take a look around you, does it seem that way? While the Fair Labor Standards Act of 1940 still states that our work weeks should be limited to 40 hours, the average worker puts in about 47.[12] And that's not even the worst part. The worst part is that we don't need to work eight hours a day. In fact, we shouldn't.

The 40 hour work week was put into effect during the time of the Industrial Revolution, where physical labor was the main energy source. Now our main commodity is mental energy, which can't be sustained as long as physical energy. In fact, research shows that "deep work and concentration" can only be sustained for a maximum of two hours. [13] So what in the world are we doing with the other six hours a day?

Additionally, research also shows that we aren't all wired to work effectively during the same hours of the day. Due to our individual biological rhythms and hormones, it's true that some people are "morning birds" while others are "night owls". And by requiring the night owl to not only awaken but perform their best during the most unproductive stage of their day, we end up garnering less overall output. In his article, Srinivas Rao goes on to pose that, "It's possible we're missing out on people's highest levels of performance simply because we insist that people work 8 hours a day." [12]

Once the eight hour workday was created, over fifty years ago, Rao provides an explanation as to where the "9-5" came from. He states, "To support this, we built an education system in which people were conditioned into an 8-hour day. Since school ended at 3, extracurricular activities were added so people would learn to be in one place from 9am to 5pm." [12]

Recently, a financial services company in Australia, Collins SBA, implemented a five hour workday and found these results: "We have found that productivity has actually increased across the board because people are looking for clever, more effective ways of doing their job. Interestingly, we've noticed that sick leave has dropped by around 12 percent and we think that's because people have more time now to relax, more time to exercise, more time to spend with their friends and family. Likewise, employee engagement has gone up dramatically. We've run quite a few client surveys and everybody's really engaged and motivated." [14]

Can you even imagine a five hour workday? Does it seem like a dream? For some people—these employees included—it's a reality. And perhaps it will become more of a norm for other companies as well. One can hope. Even if your company never makes this switch (which is more likely), doesn't it feel reassuring to know that there is a reason behind the burnout? When you know there is science to support your after-lunch-crash and resulting coffee maker trip, you may be able to take a sigh of relief with your hazelnut blend.

Humans weren't meant to work as hard as we do. Neither our bodies nor minds are built to take the amount of stress and fatigue we put them through. So when you look at how much your medical coverage costs, keep this in mind: we are doing this to ourselves. We are plaguing ourselves, and to what end?

Perhaps you are thinking, "I agree with you, Amy, but this system is necessary for the industry I'm in," or, "I have in-person clients and meetings that can't be accomplished in that time frame," or, "I work in a hospital where people need constant care." Unfortunately, I know that. I am in one of those industries as well. Until the government decides on different school hours, I will be stuck in the eight hour cycle as well.

So, instead of wishing for the perfection of a shorter workday or a flexible schedule, try to enjoy the time you are there. There are dozens of small changes you can make to help ease your mind and body instead of running them into the ground:

- Get a fresh cup of coffee and drink it hot from top to bottom
- Take two minutes every hour to do some breathing and/or stretching
- Put calming music on in the background
- Eat lunch outside
- Do some yoga in or out of your seat
- Dance

Who cares if you work in a cubicle and everyone one else is quietly sitting at their desks for all eight plus hours? You have the ability to take control of your circumstances—you just have to be willing to be different.

If you are bold, you can get your body and mind in the right space. And while you may be afraid that people will judge you, they will often be impressed and wish they could follow your lead. I have my own office, but even people I don't know will stop by to enjoy my essential oil diffuser and remark about how calm my space is. And if they took similar steps, they could change their situation as well.

Ok, so now that we've dealt with the opinions of your co-workers, what about your boss? More often than not, as long as you get your work done, they won't care. But if they do, is that someone you really want answer to for 40-47 of your 112 weekly waking hours?

And if they care enough to bring it up to you, you can always show them the research behind any of these methods. It's there. Being aware of the body-mind connection not only reaps positive benefits, but I believe it's necessary for our survival. We can only push so hard until something breaks.

Margin

My search for red leaf lettuce seemed like it would never end. We changed grocery stores when we moved and unfortunately this new one did not have as good of a produce selection. In fact, some days it didn't even have a complete one. Many times I would graze the aisles of empty shelves, trying to find anything edible.

Now, for most produce, I can manage with something else or go to with the frozen option, but red leaf lettuce is different.

I take the same lunch to work everyday; red leaf lettuce salad. That's one of my few routines, and I cling to it. It took me a year to find a consistent lunch that I liked, kept me full, and made me feel energized. So not being able to find the main ingredient was unbearably frustrating, causing outbursts and breakdowns on multiple occasions. Outbursts over red leaf lettuce? Yes. It may seem like a small problem, but when small problems happen weekly, they turn into big problems. And I had hit my breaking point.

At first, I did what most people would do—I asked an employee.

It didn't go so well.

> Me: "Excuse me, do you have anymore red
> leaf lettuce?"
>
> Employee: "Go home."
>
> Me: "What?"
>
> Employee: "Produce go home."
>
> Translation: The produce people had gone
> home for the day.

Ok, I'll try again next week.

When I came back the next week, the same exchange ensued.

After this, I started taking my grocery shopping trips in the morning instead of the evening, knowing I'd seen produce people around at this time.

The first time I tried this, it worked splendidly. Upon my request, a big, beautiful head of red leaf lettuce was brought out.

Maybe you can't appreciate that now, but perhaps once you've made multiple unsuccessful trips before and after work, you will.

This search also produced more human interaction within a grocery store than I'd had since that lady tried to recruit me for her pyramid scheme job. When it comes to grocery shopping, I have the get-in-quick-get-out-quicker mentality. I'm the one wearing AirPods who goes to the self check out with a full cart. Why? This busy area breeds busy people. One of the ways I try to avoid that stress is to get out of busy places as fast as possible.

That being said, you can see how important it was for me to specifically have red leaf lettuce. But again, why? Some of you may be thinking, "Uh, Amy, there is more than one kind of lettuce; why is this even a problem?"

Well, Romaine lettuce is intermittently being recalled. Green leaf lettuce is too tough and bland for a whole salad. And spring mixes go bad after a few days. Have you ever smelled a bag of spring mix that's started to go bad? If you have, it's something you never forget. So I was stuck on red leaf.

In short, I'm rigid when it comes to my lettuce. It's not that there weren't other options available—it's just that there weren't any options that I could accept. And so, instead of being flexible, I decided it was worth about three extra hours of my time to find the one kind of lettuce I deemed suitable.

Now, for some items, they may be worth that time. Finding a wedding dress, for example. Or getting that quirky gift your friend would love. But for the majority of things, it just doesn't matter. We just don't know that.

What we do know is what we want—and we want it now. We are continually searching for the best, even though we know deep down we won't find it in stuff; even if it eats up endless hours of our time to acquire the stuff we think we have to own. And marketers know this. It's why department stores have sales for every holiday that has ever existed (President's Day Sale? Really?). It's why Black Friday exists. It's why people waste days of their lives camping out in front of Apple stores for the new iPhone. We just aren't content with what we have.

What we forget is that once we have that newly acquired thing, we still want more. In fact, it's been proven that once our basic needs are met (ie. food, water, shelter, Wifi), any improvement in other areas of our lives only adds a marginal level of happiness. And yet, such a large part of our lives are dedicated to this incremental increase.

When that first beautiful head of lettuce was gone, I had to return to the store the next week for more. Unfortunately, the odds of finding red leaf lettuce every week are still the same, but now my attitude is different. I don't get so upheaved anymore. I go to the organic section and pay an extra $3 for an acceptable alternative. Butter lettuce, for example. I've learned to be flexible with my lettuce.

Though much headache and heartache ensued from this search for my perfect, I've come to the other side of it. I've learned to be content with what's in front of me instead of constantly seeking the margin of perfection.

Routine

I don't have one. Not one I like anyway. We've been in our current living situation (our first house!) for awhile and yet I still don't have a schedule of when things get done. Grocery shopping typically on the weekends. Cleaning whenever I have a free couple hours. Laundry whenever I run out of clothes. Repeat.

When I was little, my mom and dad definitely had a schedule: cleaning on Saturday, grocery shopping on Wednesday, church on Sunday. While I had a schedule too—school, homework, eat, sleep, repeat—the first time I really had agency over my whole day was college.

Though much of my day was dictated by my class schedule (no one told me you didn't have to go!), that still left many hours of the day free. But I knew this before leaving for college, so I emailed every club that I had a potential interest in to create the penultimate schedule. And it was pretty good. No hour was left unspent. Every day of the week consisted of class and club meetings. Except Friday.

Friday was for Ultimate Frisbee, Soccer games, and game nights. That was actually the best schedule I can remember having. Because I had so few responsibilities, I spent the rest of my time doing what I loved: activities, music, volunteering.

After dorm life, though, came more responsibility.

I moved into an off-campus house during my second semester of my sophomore year. While I knew the other ladies in the house, I didn't know how much harder living off campus would be. I didn't know how much work it took to prepare your own food for a week, and then clean up said food preparation. I also didn't know that no one else in the house cleaned the shared spaces, which, in this house, were many. The kitchen. The dining room. The living room. The sunroom. The bathrooms. So if I wanted any of that done, I had to do it myself. Sometimes I did, but other times I let it go, telling myself that it wasn't all me who made the mess so it shouldn't be all me who cleaned it up.

After college came many address changes. Two in grad school. One during my first job. One before getting married. And the last to buy our first place. Each came with a new routine, a new normal. And since I barely lived in each place long enough to see a new calendar year, I never got used to a routine. I would form habits. When to cook. When to eat. When to grocery shop. When to climb. When to see friends. But then those would break once I moved on. It seemed that just as I was getting comfortable, life shifted.

The past eight years have felt like a stage of constant change. College. Moving. Graduate school. Moving. My first full-time job. Moving. Getting married. Buying a house. Moving again. Getting a pup. Thinking about moving.

Of course, all of these changes were exciting and chosen, they just now seem like a lot to cram into such a small span of time.

So here we are at our new place. Six months in, I hung our pictures. After ten months, we had each room organized for its intended purpose. Though we don't have a "disaster room" anymore, we are still in transition. And yet, I feel as though I've been in transition for the past eight years. When will life ever feel "normal"? When will I feel "at home"? When will I settle into a predictable and stable existence?

It seems that while everyone else is tired of normalcy, I dream of it. I hope for the day where my next week is predictable and settled. On Sunday, I go to the grocery store. On Thursday, I go out for coffee with friends. On Saturday, I hike.

Routines are good. They are necessary to maintain balance and order. But I wonder if intensely focusing on them is a good thing afterall. Am I just clinging to them as my next savior, when in fact I need something else?

Life isn't predictable at any stage. You have to seize what's given to you. You have to embrace the unpredictable and navigate it with the mundane. You have to balance the spectacular with the mediocre. And when you are able to accept this uncertainty, you allow life to catch you up in it's beautiful mystery.

Yes, I would love to predict exactly what's to come. I ache to answer the questions which plague my mind. Will I have kids? Will I make it back to Zion, and Bryce, and the Grand Canyon? Will I ever have a job that I adore? Will I live in a place that I finally call home?

But instead of micromanaging all the details, I want to let life happen instead of planning it all. And that's hard. It means cutting back. It means losing control. But it also means getting to experience more.

Blu

Wake up. Pee. Eat. Sleep. Walk. Pee. Poo. Eat. Sleep. Repeat.

The definition of a simple life, right?

Not when you are meshing that life into events of your own

Wake up. Get dressed. Makeup. Walk dog. Feed dog. Feed self. Coffee. Drive to work. Work. Grocery store. See friends. Walk dog. Feed dog. Feed self. Cycle. Sleep.

The first week we got Blu, I had time off for Spring Break. This turned out to be necessary, as he required constant attention and care. So the majority of my time was spent with him. I couldn't go out and "get things done" or he would get anxious at home alone. I had to put down the computer when he wanted to snuggle. I stopped listening to podcasts during the day so I could listen incase he peed in the house. And even as I did less, I felt myself gaining more. More time spent in the present. More hours noticing simple beauties. More hours just generally awake. More hours aware of another being and his needs above my own.

It is so easy to get weighed down by what we "need" to do. I "need" to exercise today. I "need" take this extra job. I "need" to go to this happy hour. But if we replaced need with want, our lives would be much richer. I want to do this core HIIT today. I want to take on another client. I want to spend time with these friends. And if you can't say that you want to do it, then don't. Own that. Know that you have agency over certain hours of your day and take responsibility for what and who you fill them with.

Halfway through that first week of having Blu, I replaced need with want. I want to wake up early and get my day started. I want to sit outside for an hour while I wait for him to pee. I want to spend hours snuggling this formerly neglected doggo. These simple semantics helped me to reshape my thoughts, and in doing so my choices became privileges instead of obligations.

Our year of having Blu hasn't been easy. In fact, it's been downright difficult. I've never had a dog with anxiety before, and it's been hard. I've never had a dog run away from me multiple times, and it's been hard. I've never had a dog who needs such constant attention, guidance, and distraction, and it's been super hard.

But he's also been the best. He makes us laugh out loud daily. He's such a good cuddler. He's learning how to chill and not be on guard all the time. And so am I. Because he is proof that it's the hard things that are the most valuable.

So I'm letting go of my expectations of the perfect dog. I'm laying down my definition of good. I'm accepting the reality of who Blu is instead of who I want him to be. And he is better than perfection.

Math

We are a DINK household: Dual Income No Kids. Besides our fur-baby. Basically, we have steady incomes and minimal expenses. That being said, I work at a non-profit school for kids with disabilities, so I pick up other jobs here and there. Regardless, we have zero debt, minus our mortgage, and all it takes is math.

I've never had debt in my life. Maybe that seems elitist or privileged, but it's actually just math. Growing up, money was very tight in my family. Thus, I learned early that things cost money and if I wanted them, I needed to get them myself. So I did. I started babysitting and dog walking when I was 12. I got my first paycheck when I was 14. All throughout high school and college I was employed every month of the year.

I also developed lots of interests and hobbies that didn't require money: hiking, volunteering, music. I picked sports that didn't require much equipment: volleyball and track. And when something arose that I wanted to do or have, I paid for it. In cash.

That kind of mindset not only allowed me to discover lots of ways to have fun for free, but also allowed me to never open a credit card. I honestly didn't understand the difference between a debit card and credit card until well into college. Ok, maybe grad school. I just couldn't wrap my head around the fact that people would use money that they didn't have. I do understand the concept for cars or houses, but for department store trips? What could you possibly want in a mall that you can't pay for today? If you have an answer to that question, that's incorrect.

What you spend money on reveals what you value.

I get it—we want stuff. We want it now! But at what cost? Though I've never been in the shoes of someone trying to scrape together the money to pay off their credit card debt, I can sympathize what they might be feeling, and no handbag or watch is worth that. What unbearable stress and turmoil we put ourselves through for stuff. For stuff that doesn't last. For stuff that starts to lose both it's extrinsic and intrinsic value the moment we walk outside the store with it.

On his radio talk show about finance, Dave Ramsey talks about this constant state of want and debt we live in. During one show, he stated, "People are trying to take your freedom from you by forcing you to conform." Instead of investing in what we truly want, we often let others determine our values. And then those really aren't our values at all.

Did you know that there are websites where people give away their (very nice) stuff for free? Did you know that there are thrift stores where the clothes are just as nice as new ones, and half the price? Did you know that there are communities in the world (and even America) that exist purely on the barter economy? Now, as an aspiring minimalist, I'm not advocating for you to continue to fill up your life with stuff, but I am saying that if you do find yourself in need of clothes, shoes, furniture, books, dishes, board games, and/or tools, there are other options than buying them new.

You aren't a lesser person if you shop at Goodwill. In fact, when you add up the environmental, social, and financial impact of buying used over new, the benefits far outweigh the negatives.

- You're missing the play-doh in Cranium that you'd throw away anyway.

- You have to wash that shirt before you wear it for the first time.

- You always have to wear socks with these particular sneakers.

Now let's look at the positives:

• You have more money to spend on other necessities.

• You have more time not worrying about paying off those items.

• You decrease the pollution that factories exhaust to make that item new.

• You increase recycling.

• You save a perfectly good item from sitting in a landfill for the next 20 years.

• You save your future self from stress and anxiety.

See? More positives.

Now, I know that I'm missing a big piece of the equation: people's opinions. A huge reason that we buy things new isn't necessarily about the monetary impact, but the social one. People won't notice your "new shoes" that already have a scuff mark on the side. People won't do a double-take when your car goes driving by without that glossy shine. People won't compliment you on your new couch that's obviously been sat upon countless times. But, as FDR's presidential advisor, Bernard Baruch, stated about his dinner party seating arrangements: "Those who mind don't matter, and those who matter don't mind." [15]

How freeing it would be if we lived like we believed that.

Graded

When I was in high school, I worked for grades. I don't remember why or what sparked that desire. As a kid, good grades got me dinner at my favorite restaurant for grilled cheese and french fries. But as I grew older, the rewards were more intrinsic than extrinsic. So, no matter the subject, I strove for an A.

English was my love. I enjoyed getting As. I liked doing the work. Math was not. So while I could have "settled" for a B or C, I didn't. Since the homework made no sense to me, I did hours of it until I broke down crying. I remember nights where I had to go to bed before the homework was finished because of how out of control and exhausted I felt. But I was up the next morning at 5:00am with my dad to finish it. And for what? To get a grade. Not for an education. It was Discrete Math—what was I ever going to use that for? Absolutely nothing.

College was similar. Though my many hobbies kept me too busy to get As in every class, it was still the majority grade I earned each semester. And when I didn't get an A, I thought, "What's wrong with me?"

The problem is that I never thought past the grade. I never thought, "How can I apply this? How will I use this? Do I even like this? Is this worth it?" I never asked myself which classes were worth the effort for the A and which were better left for the "Cs get degrees" mentality.

Graduate school was the same, but on steroids. The workload was incredible. It was the first time in my life that I didn't have time for a job, which made the prospect of paying for it all the more stressful. I thought about working at the climbing gym or picking up babysitting jobs, but between the homework and the internship work, I didn't have the physical or mental capacity. And in a sense, I felt like I was failing.

Some of my professors were unreasonable, and others were slightly crazy. But, come hell or high water, I completed the work. I tried to read the "required" book chapters. I bought the "mandatory" materials. I pushed myself harder than ever, and subsequently fell off the edge more than once.

If getting that A comes with an intense level of stress and anxiety, what do you think comes next? If you are hating every moment of getting that achievement, what do you think your life will look like post accomplishment? Whatever amount of work you are putting in now is equivalent to how much you will acquire later. So "settle" for a B. What you can achieve by putting in your best effort without accumulating negative side effects is the maximum you should aim for. Best does not equal perfect.

Instead of giving more time to subjects I liked, or my music, or my running, I wasted it on chasing a grade that is now meaningless.

We chase after meaningless relationships in much the same way. We want a wider circle of friends. We don't want to be alone. We "feel bad" saying no. Ultimately, we think that being with certain people will get us certain things. Popularity. Prestige. Pride. Purpose. But people don't give you these. You have to find that for yourself. And you can't do that if you are constantly distracted with others so that you can't make a decision about your time that it distinctly, solely yours.

We feel like we have to "prove ourselves" to others, but we don't. Why? Proving yourself means that you are trying to attain some positive perception from a person or group of people. And that's impossible to control. People's perceptions are different no matter what. No one is universally relevant. Some people idolize Taylor Swift and others hate her. Some people incessantly follow LeBron James' every movement while others have never heard of him.

Instead of asking, "Am I measuring up to other's standards?", ask, "What am I actually seeking?"

When I asked myself this question, these were my top three:

1. Peace

2. Joy

3. Beauty

But you have to find that around yourself first before you can appreciate it fully in other spaces and places. Notice when the world around you is still. Notice your friend's laughter. Notice the daily sunsets you are given.

Time for these appreciations is only possible once you cut out the countless other things you put ahead of your actual goals and dreams. And that takes intentionality. It takes saying no.

No

Two-year-olds love this word. Why? It has power.

After this age, we grow to hate it, as it is often used to keep us from doing the things we most want to.

"Can I get a horse?"

"Can I go to Ariel's on Friday night?"

"Can I use the car tomorrow?"

"Can I go to Zambia for the summer?"

But as I keep growing, I find that using this word regains me that power I found as a toddler.

"Can you come to this fundraiser?"

"Can you stay late to work on this project?"

"Can you come to this game?"

"Can you join my Facebook group?"

Most of these I would like to do, in isolated circumstances which don't also intersect with the other plans I've already made.

But, doing them all at once will not only burn you out, it will also singe the people around you.

In one week, one of my friends was in a male pageant on Monday, I visited my friend and her baby on Tuesday, we met up for drinks with a friend from China on Wednesday, we had community group on Thursday, and then left for a friend's wedding on Friday.

Yes— I wanted to do all these things.

Yes— they all involved people I deeply care for.

Yes— this was too much to do in one week.

No— is what I should have said to at least one of these invitations.

This isn't an isolated case. It's a weekly struggle in which one must sift between the necessary and the pseudo-obligatory; the things one must do for one's well-being and the things one thinks one must do to stay connected, achieve status, or whatever other ridiculous rationale we come up with.

Because you know what I didn't get to do that week? Read. Pray. Exercise. Breathe. Play. In going places and making plans just because I was asked to, I sacrificed time for the things which add joy to my daily life.

Living simply and in unperfection isn't about doing less so that you have time to sit around. It's about doing less so that when the opportunity for more comes, you have the time and energy to do it.

Like when I intentionally planned nothing for Memorial Day weekend. With nothing on the calendar, this is what I was able to do: hike seven and a half miles with my doggo and a good friend, stop at the winery on the way home, make a delicious, homemade brunch, set up my basement singing studio, and complete a 20 mile bike ride.

Had I planned out every hour of my weekend, as I normally do, how many of these things would I have had time for? Very few. Maybe I would've fit more in, but would I had enjoyed it as much?

When we have more, sometimes we get lost in it instead of finding ourselves. And isn't the latter what we truly want in the end?

Time

I had two appointments today. As I was about to leave for the first, I got a phone call from their office.

"We are sorry to cancel this close to the appointment, but the doctor had to go into emergency surgery."

The sad part? This is the fifth time I've gotten this call from this same doctors office.

The sadder part? I asked for this doctor since my usual doctor gets called into surgery so often that I only request her for my annual visit. I wanted a doctor who was sure to be there.

Then, about a week later, I got a call from a different doctor's office.

"Yes, we were just calling to ask if you were coming in for your appointment today,"

I replied, "No, I called this morning to reschedule for tomorrow at 11:45am."

"Oh, well the person you spoke to did not put the appointment in and now that spot is taken. Can you come in at 5:45pm?"

"No, do you have anything else in the afternoon?"

"Unfortunately not. How about Wednesday at 10:45am?"

"Yes, please put it in the calendar right now."

After I settled down from the initial frustration, these interactions got me thinking; why did this happen?

My first doctor over scheduled herself. My second doctor's office didn't take the time to reschedule my time slot. Or maybe someone walked up to the desk with a problem that required immediate attention. Maybe my appointment was inputed correctly but it didn't save correctly. Whatever the issue was, the attention to detail was lost due to a lack of time.

Why do we do this to ourselves? Why do we over schedule ourselves? Why do we negate attention to detail so often?

There are two options: either we put this strain upon ourselves, or this strain is thrust upon us.

But there is one solution: resist the strain.

Fight back against it. When you find yourself doing mental gymnastics just to get to every appointment, obligation, or chore, STOP. Determine what is truly necessary. What NEEDS to be done today. And what can wait until tomorrow. And if tomorrow is just as packed as today, then keep going through your calendar, pushing back events until it is manageable. If life can go on without you attending that event or going to that game, then don't.

Now, I'm going to let you in on a secret: busy does not equal success. Oftentimes, in fact, it yields the opposite result.

Recently, I drove 12,000 miles before getting my oil changed (that's double the recommended time). A couple months ago I got a tick bite on a Thursday but didn't get around to contacting my doctor about it until the following Tuesday night. In the same email to my doctor, I followed up on another issue that had arisen a year ago. My friend sent me his 23 page book to review and it took me a month to finish it (granted it was single spaced). All of this neglect because I fill my time up too much.

Can I go without cooking today? If you have food ready to eat, yes.

Can I skip that fundraiser? If it won't cause a rift with those who asked you to be there, yes.

Can I go without working out today? If your body says it's already tired, yes.

The only way you can seize the day is by giving yourself enough time to enjoy the minutes that make it up. And the rest you can seize tomorrow.

In her book, "Do Less. Get More", Shaa Wasmund states: "You need to be ruthless if you want to get your life back. Often we create a rod for our own back by constantly saying yes to people which means our to-do list grows out of control.... We've been conditioned to believe that a degree of stress is a good thing, it's a badge of honour that proves we must be working really hard, pushing to get the most out of life. Don't buy it. It's a myth." [16]

I realized that this was true of me. I was letting other people determine what should be important to me and thus was not taking ownership of my problems. I was allowing my problems to overwhelm me instead of facing them head on and finding enjoyment and strength in that.

So instead, I had to look at my time and my money. How I was spending those were not in line with what I wanted and said I valued. I needed to take an honest assessment and weed out the unnecessary. So I did. And you must as well. You will miss out on some opportunities. You may hurt some feelings. But you will gain more of yourself, even while it comes at the expense of being nice.

Nice

One reason that we fill up our time is because people ask it of us. And we feel that the only way to be nice is to say yes.

I spent so many years of my life being "nice". Everyone said it. My teachers, friend's parents, old ladies at church. I was generally a happy kid and never really needed to fake it. But as I got older, being nice became harder.

Growing up meant that I started to form my own ideas and opinions. I no longer rely on the way I've always done things to determine how I live my life now. I'm evolving. As I go through this process, I'm learning that being nice doesn't actually get me what I want, as it often comes at the cost of my honesty.

It can be something small: "That person just bumped into me and didn't notice,",

medium: "This conflict isn't getting resolved,",

or large: "I am being blatantly

disrespected,"

And those wrong things need to be righted.

Recently, we had some plumbing work done. Well, we were told we were having some plumbing work done. Our condo association told all homeowners that there would be week-long work occurring between the hours of 8:00am-6:00pm. Maybe this wouldn't have been so bad had we not just moved in six weeks prior. Maybe it wouldn't have been so bad if we hadn't just adopted a dog. But whatever. It was happening. So we pushed through it.

A week after the work was completed, I got a text from Adam, "Did you call a plumber to the house?"

"No,"

"Well one showed up this morning. I let him in because I thought you called him."

"Huh, that's weird. Well our hot water was taking a while to heat up. Maybe that's why he was there?"

When I got home that night, our hot water still was taking a long time to heat up. So long, in fact, that finally I realized it wasn't heating up at all. Hmm. Must be connected to the plumber that came today right? I called and the offices were closed.

Maybe the guy who did the week-long plumbing work knows? I called his cell phone.

At least he picked up. But all he knew was that the condo association company had called plumbers to some of the homes today. He thought they might be sending another plumber out that evening, but couldn't tell me anything more than that.

Okay. Who should I call? How was I to know when/if that was happening? I currently had no hot water in my house. I couldn't do the dishes. I couldn't shower. And I couldn't get an answer.

I called and emailed the condo association, but of course their offices were closed too.

So, with no other alternative, I drove to my friend's apartment and took a shower. While not the biggest deal in the world, it was still an hour out of my evening I hadn't planned on giving up. It was an inconvenience that I pay a condo fee to avoid.

And all the while no one could tell me why the problem happened and when it would be resolved.

The next morning I got an email back from the condo association:

"The plumbing issue has been fixed."

That's great. But, since I am capable of turning on the faucet and figuring that out for myself, that's not the question I was asking. I wanted to know what the problem was. Who fixed it? Why was it a problem? When it happens again, as it inevitably will, who am I to contact?

In the past, I'd try to take this instance "in stride".

"Oh well, I guess I'll just have to live with this. Just hope it doesn't happen again."

But that kind of response no longer seems acceptable to me.

I am paying this condo association large sums of money each month to cover issues like these, and this is how they operate? The kind of response that I got from the association told me that at any point I could come home to any number of small or large problems and I'm just supposed to "roll with it"?

No more Mrs. Nice Girl.

I called the condo association and had a frank but polite conversation with the representative. I told him that it was unacceptable for me to come home to no hot water and not know why. While he was able to give me a rationale for the problem and its solution, I wanted a solution to the next problem. I wanted a number I could call with a person on the other end who would answer and be able to help me. He told me that there was an emergency number I could call. And that number went straight into my contacts.

Just like you should call out people you care about to be better, you should demand more from the companies and people you deal with. And that's what I intend to do. Yes, it will be more work. Yes, it will get "awkward" and be harder to "deal with" then if I just sat back and waited for the next disaster to ensue. But I'm done accepting that crap happens without repercussions. I don't think that you have to be rude about it, but I do think that if we want situations in our lives to change, then we have to change.

Do you feel slighted by someone? Say something. Do you feel cheated? Do something. Do you feel wronged? Have that conversation.

Maybe this seems like the opposite of living in unperfection. Doesn't that just mean doing the least work possible?

No. Unperfection means having awkward conversations so you can root out negative things from your life. Unperfection means dealing with the hard things so that you can live more fully. Unperfection means accepting that some situations won't change, but it also means accepting responsibility for the situations you can change.

If you have built up resentment, hurt, or anger at people or situations, deal with it. Act upon your feelings which tell you, "This isn't right," and take the first step toward unbending your world from the grip of that negativity. Because unless it's rooted out— not just weeded—it will always have a place in your heart, and you need that space for other things to grow. Like peace. And joy. And beauty.

When you root out hatred, you allow in freedom.

Judgement

"I'm not judging you...well, maybe a little."

Who has either heard this phrase said directly to them or via someone's nonverbal cues? All of us, I'm sure. And, we've all also been on the other side of the equation. We all like to say that we "aren't judging", but that's not true.

More importantly: who cares? People will always judge you. When they say, "I'm not judging you" what they really mean is, "I'm ok with you making a choice different than mine." Like in "The Princess Bride", when Wesley says, "As you wish", what he really meant was, "I love you".

People don't always say what they mean, but once we are able to understand the unspoken meaning, we can communicate more effectively.

Because we can't help but judge. We are wired to have opinions and the basis of our opinion means that we disagree with the opposite. So, if you find someone who believes the opposite of your belief and you say, "It's fine, I'm not judging," that's not true. You certainly are judging. You just want to say something that makes it seem as though you still somehow affirm their life choices. But you don't! So stop saying you aren't judging. You are.

If you approve of everything, you stand for nothing.

The good thing is, the people who judge you and still like you will stick around. The ones that don't, won't, and you should be happy to see them go. Part of the reason we judge is because whatever we believe, we see that as the best. Everything else is subpar. So, by proxy, if someone you like is living a subpar life, you'd like to right that for them. Part of judgement is love. If you judge someone, you care. If you didn't care, you wouldn't give the person enough time to judge them.

But just because you know people will judge you, don't let that judgement determine your decisions. We make so many choices because we don't want to be judged. We give to charities we don't particularly care about. We go to every event we are invited to because we don't want to be left out or seem rude. We hide truths we believe because we'd rather people have opinions of us that are more palatable. But in doing so, we rob ourselves of truly being known.

Don't fear judgment. You can't be everyone's definition of perfect, and that means you will be judged. Instead, accept judgement as a fact of life—even as a good thing—because it means people truly care about you. But don't bow to it either. Don't allow your choices to be predestined for you by someone else. Ultimately, you call the shots. You choose how to spend the hours that make up your day and the resources you are given. And until you allow yourself freedom from judgment of others, you can't live honestly.

I wish we didn't have to start sentences with "honestly". Why don't we expect people to be honest with us from the beginning without noting it? Why do we breathe a sigh of relief or feel a genuine connection when someone says, "Can I be honest?" Yes. Why are we anything but?

Even if after the "honestly" comes something biting or hard to swallow, we should be grateful at the chance to truly know someone and be known rather than be spared for our feelings. We are all better when we are honest, and we are made better when

others are honest with us. Even at the cost of feeling judged.

Introvert

I was talking with a co-worker the other day about a great supervisor he once had. As he summarized this person who had so many wonderful qualities, one thing in particular stuck out. Not because it was unusual—I hear this quality toted as a major positive all the time—but because of how readily we accept this as a good quality. He said, "She just loves people."

Of course that's good. Somethings wrong with you if you don't love people, right?

I think when we say, "They just love people," we mean, "They love being around people," including: people they genuinely love, people they tolerate, and strangers. If you are a "people-person", you are energized by people. In short, you are an extrovert.

But what if you don't love people? What if being around people exhausts and stresses you out—even people who you like? What if you get energy from being by yourself and not with other people? I guess if "loving people" is a good quality, then "getting exhausted by people" is bad quality, right?

In church, whenever we have greeting time, the pastor gives two options. If you are friendly, here's some time to talk with people. If talking with strangers makes you cringe, go get some coffee, use the bathroom, or take time to look at the Worship Guide. Depending on how the second option is presented, people may politely laugh. Why? To diffuse the tension? To make others believe that we aren't one of those unfriendly people? Or do we just laugh awkwardly because more of us would rather not admit that we don't "love people", but we think this makes us rude?

Introversion doesn't make you rude. It doesn't make you a weirdo. It makes you one of 16-50% of people who don't like people. [17] And that's ok.

Now current research is trending toward a theory that more of us are not on the extreme ends of the spectrum (either introverts or extroverts), but rather somewhere along the spectrum as Ambiverts. So, not everyone who considers themselves an introvert wants to be alone all the time, and not everyone who considers themselves an extrovert needs to be around people all the time. We all have tendencies that lean more one way than the other, but it's not all or nothing. That would be lunacy. [18]

But here's why this matters. Our culture praises those with more extroverted tendencies and shames the introverts. Those who are the loudest and most vibrant get the social media presence and prestige in their careers. Those who are quieter and more thoughtful get passed over for promotions. Those with more friends are popular. Those with few, deep connections don't get on the invite list.

These facts lead some to develop more extroverted tendencies. When I went to college, I shed my shy skin and dove into the world of "new friends" and opportunities. I became more vocal. I signed up for clubs, took leadership roles, and got a job where I called the shots. And I loved it. At that time in my life, I truly was energized by people and sought them out.

But after college, I was drained. I craved time alone, or with just a few people for company. I gave all my time to everyone else for four years and now I needed some for myself.

I still find myself doing this today. I sign up for volunteer opportunities, only to fall off after a few months of service. I take on work after my 40 hours, only to quit before the year is through. And it's not that I can't do these things. But all of these opportunities put me in positions where I have to interact with even more people than I normally would in a given week, and that's exhausting for me. That's stressful. It's why I take so many naps. It's probably why I get sick so often. And I need to learn to stop. I need to learn to find a balance.

We don't all need to be extroverts. Being an extrovert doesn't make you better and being an introvert doesn't make you worse. We are all equal. The pressure to be an extrovert adds so much weight to someone who isn't naturally inclined that way, so take the pressure off. Acknowledge your strengths and weakness and own them. You will find yourself less stressed and more at peace.

Having hundreds of friends won't make you happy. Getting invited to every event won't make you feel fulfilled. Being an extrovert isn't the only perfect path. So if the people you love are few vs. the masses, love them well. And leave everyone else to the

extroverts.

Failure

This can take a lot of forms. I didn't even realize that I was scared of it until I started this process of becoming an unperfectionist. And then I realized that failure is one of my greatest fears. I always want to be prepared, which is a good thing. But not when it comes at the expense of my sanity.

Fear of failure is why I had anxiety for two months before starting middle school and cried to my mom every night. It's why I started having panic attacks misdiagnosed as IBS. It's why I had my first migraine on my first day of my first job. It's why I started having vertigo during one of the most stressful times of my life. Often, the fear can be more debilitating than the actual failure.

No one ever told me that you won't be perfect at something the first time you try it, or the fourth, or twelfth, or hundredth. Well, maybe someone did tell me, but I didn't listen. So when I started something new, I usually quit it, unless I was naturally good at it, like singing. Anything that was hard—like volleyball, or track, or ultimate frisbee—I quit.

Being a Speech-Language Pathologist allows me to seek out certain populations of interest and explore them. That means I have to do something for the first time a lot, like feeding therapy. This was an area that interested me since college, but I didn't have any experience in it. Thus, I had to forge my own path toward learning more to treat it effectively. That meant doing research. And then it meant treating my first client.

I was so nervous in the weeks leading up to it. Though I had a general idea of what to do, I researched it for hours beforehand. I went down rabbit holes much too deep for what I was dealing with. But I wanted to be prepared. I wanted to be versed. When people asked me questions, I needed to have THE answer. "I don't know," was never an option.

What I didn't know is the greatest antidote to failure is action. Because the more you do something, the better you get at it. Duh. But if you think you're supposed to be perfect at it the first time and you aren't, then you think that you are a failure.

So I had my first two feeding clients. While they each required skilled therapy, neither one was more than I could handle. My current knowledge as a clinician prepared me for the first steps, and anything more I learned by actually doing things in the moment, not listening to an hour long lecture online. I'm sure that material was helpful, but I could've definitely gotten by without it.

During my first year of practicing, I felt like I was failing a lot at the school where I worked. But oddly enough, no one else felt that way. No one cared that I wasn't perfect. And once I was able to accept that and believe it, I became a better therapist.

As the kids were learning, I was learning. I learned which strategies worked and which didn't. I learned which reading comprehension tricks stuck and which flopped. I learned which materials were helpful and which bombed. How? By attempting, tweaking, and ultimately figuring it out. By succeeding, and by failing.

If you can let go of your fear of failure, you will find peace. Because ultimately, stress is the result of fear.

When we fear, we feel stress. This often happens when we play the "if, then" game. If I don't get this done in time, then I will get in trouble. If I do this wrong, then there could be negative consequences. If I don't get these errands done in time, then I'll get stuck in traffic and dinner will be late.

So many times we don't pursue a dream or a goal because of the fear of failure. What if I forget the words and this audition goes south? What if the supervisor is mean and this job interview ends in a "no"? What if I show up and don't know anyone on this kickball team?

Instead of letting the "what ifs" rule you, combat them with the "so whats". So what if you don't get the part? So what if it's not the job for you? So what if you're the odd (wo)man out? It's ok. When you remember that there is no perfect, it allows you to open yourself up to the possibility of failure, and then it doesn't seem so scary.

In fact, I would challenge you to fail. Go do something that you know you will tank. Go try to run 10 miles when you know you can't jog one. Go make a soufflé when you can't even crack an egg.

Go paint a canvas you know will look like Picasso, but worse. When you give yourself the permission to fail, you find that it's not so bad. It doesn't ruin your life. And then it doesn't have to own you.

Failure is part of life, learning, and growth. Instead of fearing it, embrace it. For failing is the only way to improve and eventually succeed.

Unperfection

We are conditioned to crave perfection. We are born with a desire for it. But it isn't possible. It isn't attainable. And living in pursuit of it leaves you even further from it. In fact, we sacrifice a lot in pursuit of perfection: time, relationships, joy, experiences, hope, laughter, rest, beauty.

We need to allow ourselves to be human. We need to remove the stigma that comes with our humanity. Because part of being human is unperfection.

So let go. Give up. Get Bs. Fail. Fall. Discern. Be quiet. Be grateful. Be present. Rest. Breathe. Live.

You have to control your stress and anxiety. You have to decide to be calm. No one is going to do that for you. In fact, lots of people are going to try to steal your peace and joy from you. Life will always present you with stress, but you get to choose how you respond to it. You get to decide if it owns you. Don't let it.

The hope and truth is that it's possible to eradicate. And where there's hope, there's action. And where there's action there's change. And where there's change, there's healing.

So how do we combat it? How do we win this fight?

The answer is simple.

Do less. Live more. Embrace unperfection.

Notes

1. Herbert Bayard Swope Quotes (Author of Inside the German Empire; In the Third Year of the War)." Goodreads. https://www.goodreads.com/author/quotes/2333810.Herbert_Bayard_Swope.

2. Fox, Maggie. "More Teens, Young Adults Get Depression Diagnoses, Insurance Co Finds." NBC News. May 10, 2018. https://www.nbcnews.com/health/health-news/major-depression-rise-among-everyone-new-data-shows-n873146.

2. Columbia University's Mailman School of Public Health. "Depression is on the rise in the US, especially among young teens." ScienceDaily. www.sciencedaily.com/releases 2017/10/171030134631.htm (accessed December 27, 2018).

3. Hidaka, Brandon H. "Depression as a Disease of Modernity: Explanations for Increasing Prevalence." Journal of Affective Disorders 140, no. 3 (January 12, 2012): 205-14. doi:10.1016/j.jad.2011.12.036.

4. Asano, Evan. "How Much Time Do People Spend on Social Media?[Infographic]". Social Media Today. January 04, 2017. www.socialmediatoday.com/marketing/how-much-time-do-people-spend-social-media-infographic

5. Lewis, C. S. "Mere Christianity: A Revised and Enlarged Edition, with a New Introduction, of the Three Books, the Case for Christianity, Christian Behaviour, and Beyond Personality." New York: Macmillan Pub., 1984.

6. Przybylski, Andrew K., Murayama, Kou, Dehaan, Cody R., and Gladwell, Valerie. "Motivational, Emotional, and Behavioral Correlates of Fear of Missing out." Computers in Human Behavior 29, no. 4. April 09, 2013: 1841-848. doi:10.1016/j.chb.2013.02.014.

7. Baker, Eric. "How to Overcome FOMO: Fear of Missing Out." Time. June 07, 2016. Accessed December 27, 2018. http://time.com/4358140/overcome-fomo/.

8. Texas A&M University. "FOMO: It's your life you're missing out on."ScienceDaily.www.sciencedaily.com/releases/2016/03/160330135623.htm. (accessed December 27, 2018).

9. Milyavskaya, Marina, Saffran, Mark., Hope, Nora. et al. Motiv Emot (2018) 42: 725. https://doi.org/10.1007/s11031-018-9683-5

10. Kubu, Cynthia, & Machado, Andre. "Why Multitasking Is Bad for You." Time. April 20, 2017. http://time.com/4737286/multitasking-mental-health-stress-texting-depression/

11. Pattison, Kermit. "Worker, Interrupted: The Cost of Task Switching." Fast Company. July 28, 2008. https://www.fastcompany.com/944128/worker-interrupted-cost-task-switching

12. Ward, Marguerite. "A brief history of the 8-hour workday, which changed how Americans work." CNBC Make It. May 03, 2017. https:/www.cnbc.com/2017/05/03/how-the-8-hour-workday-changed-how-americans-work.html

13. Rao, Srinivas. "8 Reasons the 8 Hour Workday Doesn't Make Sense." The Mission – Medium. October 02, 2017. https://medium.com/the-mission/8-reasons-the-8-hour-workday-doesnt-make-sense-cde67f2e785c

14. Anand, Anu., & Craig, Victoria. "The results of ditching an 8-hour workday are"breathtaking," according to one boss." Marketplace. July 06, 2018. https://www.marketplace.org/2018/07/06/business/results-ditching-eight-hour-workday-breathtaking-according-one-boss

15. Bernard Baruch. (n.d.). https://en.wikiquote.org/wiki/Bernard_Baruch

16. Wasmund, Shaa. "Do less, get more: How to work smart and live life your way." London: Penguin Life, 2016

17. Buettner, Dan. "Are Extroverts Happier Than Introverts?". Psychology Today. May 14, 2012. https://www.psychologytoday.com/us/blog/thrive/201205/are-extroverts-happier-introverts

18. Beaton, C. "The Majority of People Are Not Introverts or Extroverts Introverts and extroverts exist, but they're exceptions and face disadvantages." Psychology Today. October 06, 2017.https://www.psychologytoday.com/us/blog/the-gen-y-guide/201710/the-majority-people-are-not-introverts-or-extroverts

Made in the USA
Middletown, DE
22 February 2019